Nala's World

written by
Dean Nicholson

illustrated by
Frann Preston-Gannon

wren
&rook

High up in the Bosnian mountains, where the earth meets the sky, there was a lonely little kitten.

That kitten was me, **Nala.**

I longed for a friend to play with, and I imagined the adventures
we could have and the places we'd see. But it always seemed like
a dream too big for a little kitten, like me. Until one day,
I looked out at the winding road and saw a man
on a bike coming towards me.

This was my chance to have the adventure I dreamed of!
So, I ran and ran alongside the bike, going as fast
as my little legs would take me.

And just as I was about to give up . . .

. . . the bike came to a stop!

The man peered down and put his face close to mine.

His name was **Dean**.
He was kind and very gentle when he ruffled my coat.

THIS was the friend
I'd been looking for.

Dean scooped me up and put me on his bike. This was it! I was about to start my adventure.

The first thing Dean did
was take me to the vet.
Although I was small,
the vet said I was strong.

And that meant I could get
my very own passport. Now I
could go wherever Dean went.

But first, we had to get to know
each other. So, I taught Dean how
to climb trees . . .

and he was there
to catch me when
I got a bit *too* brave.

I taught Dean how to playfight . . .

and that breakfast is best when it's served bright and early.

Dean showed me things too. Things I never imagined a cat could do . . . like paddling out to sea! The water was deep and scary, but Dean always looked after me.

I trusted him and he trusted me.

And so, we set off to travel the world together.

We cycled across mountains,

we camped in the woods,

we watched the sunset on the beach

and rode into towns.

Everywhere we went, people wanted to say hello.

I loved being out on the road,
but there was one thing I
wasn't made for . . .

RAIN!

I got soaked through in the storm, which made me poorly.

After that, Dean and I decided that we were in no rush to get across the world.

Looking after each other was the most important thing.

Then, one day we found a tiny puppy cowering underneath an orange tree. She was all alone, just like I had been. And she was poorly and thin.

We knew we had to help her.
The problem was we only had a small bike . . .

. . . but somehow it was
big enough for three!

With some love and care,
the puppy soon felt much
better. We named her
Balou and found a lovely
family to adopt her.

Meeting Balou taught Dean and I that it wasn't enough to just look after one another, we needed to **look after others too**.

From that moment on, wherever we went, we helped
the animals we met in any way we could. We volunteered
at animal sanctuaries and rescue centres in lots of countries.

We even started sharing photos of our adventures online, making friends thousands of miles away.

The more we helped, the more others helped too.
Before long, we were helping all sorts of
animals find their forever homes.

Today, Dean and I continue our journey on two wheels, seeing incredible places, making friends and trying to make a difference. I dreamed of finding just one friend, but now I have friends all over the world.

AMERICA

GERMANY

THAILAND

I'm one little cat with a whole friendship pack who's off on a **VERY big adventure.**

Helping Animals in Need

There are around 600 million stray animals living around the world today and most are dogs and cats. Without safe homes, these animals can get cold, hungry, lonely and sometimes poorly. But there are lots of things you can do to help!

If you find a stray dog or cat...

It can be tempting to scoop up a stray dog or cat for a cuddle, but it's best to keep your distance at first, especially if the animal seems hurt. Here are some things you can do to help:

Find out if it's a lost pet

The first thing to do is to ring the local vet or animal shelter, as they will be able to help find out if the animal has an owner. Lots of animals have microchips with their owner's contact details. If it doesn't have a microchip, you could help by making 'found pet' posters and asking a grown-up to talk to your neighbours and check social media.

Help the animal to find a new home

Most vets and animal rescue charities, such as the RSPCA, SSPCA or USPCA, will be able to look after the animal until they find it a safe, new home.

Adopting an animal

Adopting a stray from a rescue centre is one of the best ways to make a homeless animal's life better, and a rescue animal will change your life just as much as you'll be changing theirs! It's a big responsibility though – ask your family to help you find out how to look after your new pet properly.

Support a local rescue centre

If you can't care for a pet at home, that doesn't mean you can't help animals in need. Rescue centres do incredible work and are sure to be glad of any help you can give. Why not ask a grown-up to help you find your nearest animal rescue centre, and ask if you can raise some money for them?

For wee Jack ♥
D.N.

For my own lovely feline, Poe
F.P.G

First published in Great Britain in 2022 by Wren & Rook

Text copyright © Dean Nicholson, 2022. Illustration copyright © Frann Preston-Gannon, 2022

A CIP catalogue record for this book is available from the British Library.

HB ISBN: 978 1 5263 6474 6   PB ISBN: 978 1 5263 6473 9

Printed and bound in China

Picture acknowledgements: All pictures were taken by
the author Dean Nicholson from his own collection.

10 9 8 7 6 5 4 3 2

Wren & Rook
An imprint of Hachette Children's Group
Part of Hodder & Stoughton
Carmelite House , 50 Victoria Embankment, London EC4Y 0DZ

An Hachette UK Company
www.hachette.co.uk   www.hachettechildrens.co.uk